INTENTIONAL PARENTING

Family Discipleship by Design

Tad Thompson
Cruciform Press | Released February, 2011

This book is dedicated to Abby and Josiah.
My greatest prayer is for you to treasure Jesus more
than anything else in this world.
– Tad Thompson

CruciformPress

"Here is a practical page-turner that encourages fathers to engage the hearts of their families with truth and grace. In an age when truth is either ignored or despised, it is refreshing to see a book written for ordinary fathers who want their families to be sanctified by the truth . Thompson writes with a grace which reminds us that parenting flows from the sweet mercies of Christ."

Joel Beeke, President, Puritan Reformed Theological Seminary

"As parents, we know God has given us the responsibility to train our children in his ways. But many parents don't know where or how to start. Tad has done us all a favor by identifying seven key categories of biblical teaching we can utilize in teaching our children godly truth and principles. This easy-to-follow plan will help any parent put the truth of God's Word into their children's hearts."

Kevin Ezell, President, North American Mission Board, Southern Baptist Convention; father of six

"Need an introductory text for parents to the topic of discipling children? Here is a clear, simple book on family discipleship, centered on the gospel rather than human successes or external behaviors."

Timothy Paul Jones, Ph.D., Professor of Discipleship and Family Ministry, The Southern Baptist Theological Seminary

"Are you doing what you can to make sure the coming generation will praise the Lord? This book can help you in that great task. May the Lord use it powerfully."

James M. Hamilton, Ph.D, Associate Professor of Biblical Theology, The Southern Baptist Theological Seminary

"This approach is creative, thoroughly biblical, and a must read for any parent who desires for their children to love God with all their heart, soul, and might. This is a great strategy for anyone looking for a way to pull their family together around God's Word."

Blake Gideon, Senior Pastor, First Baptist Church, Inola, Oklahoma

Table of Contents

Print ISBN: 978-1-936760-06-0
ePub ISBN: 978-1-936760-10-7
Mobipocket ISBN: 978-1-936760-09-1

CruciformPress.com
email: info@CruciformPress.com
Twitter: @CruciformPress

One
THE NEED

Look

I can see the room as if it were yesterday. Metal folding chairs, flannel board, musty carpet, and all my church buddies gathered for the weekly ritual of Sunday School. As I leaned back against the wall in my chair, I had no sense there was anything unique about this particular lesson. It was simply another hour with my friends, listening to a story I had heard a thousand times before. And this is no exaggeration; I had heard the simple gospel message at least one thousand times. My dad, a Baptist pastor, was faithful to share the gospel, my mom was faithful to talk to me about the gospel, and our church was faithful in its proclamation of the gospel. I had heard the message of the cross time and time again, so when my first-grade Sunday School teacher began to tell it again that day, it seemed like an old, broken-in ball cap, very comfortable and familiar.

But something was unique about this particular

lesson; the Holy Spirit began to work in my heart. From one moment to the next, something changed. I realized in an entirely new way that the cross was about my sin, and that this all-too-familiar story demanded a response. I was undone, convicted of my sin. I spent the rest of the day thinking about Jesus hanging on the cross, dying, his sacrifice paying for what I had done. I vividly remember lying in bed that evening praying a simple, child-like prayer to God, asking him to forgive my sins. This was not the grandest of all confessions. It was not theologically precise or soteriologically accurate. But it was wrought by the Holy Spirit, who had gently and persuasively led me, a six-year-old boy, to the cross of the Savior.

I reflect often on that Sunday, and cherish it as the day I was born again by the power of the Holy Spirit working through the proclamation of the gospel. When I ponder that day, it is obvious to me that two groups were vital to my conversion and subsequent discipleship: my parents and the local church.

God intends for a beautiful partnership to exist between the home and the local church. As a matter of fact, God intends for the Christian home to be the body of Christ in microcosm. As George Whitefield once put it, "[E]very house…a little Parish, every Governor a Priest, every Family a Flock…"[1]

But historically it has been rare for the Christian

home to function even remotely like a little church. As I think about my childhood friends who were with me in that Sunday School class, I do not believe many of them were afforded the blessing of being discipled by their parents. Few of them are active in the church today.

The Situation

I have served on a church staff as a student pastor, as an associate pastor with oversight of adult education, and now as a lead pastor. At every stage of my seventeen-year experience in ministry, the disconnect between parents and children with respect to the discipleship process has become increasingly evident. The hard fact is that fathers and mothers are not taking on the responsibility to disciple their own children, and churches are doing very little, if anything, to challenge this reality. One look at my Facebook page demonstrates the painful fact that many young adults who were once quite active in student ministry programs have left the church and are questioning their faith. A young man found my Facebook account and wrote, "I just want to let you know that I don't believe in organized religion anymore. I'm not even sure I believe in God."

Personal experiences do not prove societal trends, but current research demonstrates that this young man's experience is not uncommon. Polling has shown that, of adults in their twenties who attended church as teenagers, 61 percent no longer do so.[2]

During the past thirty years, the Church has become increasingly geared towards the consumer. Pastors and church-growth experts have thought of every way imaginable to compel the masses, through attractive facilities and programs, to at least walk in the door. Often the motive is a genuine desire to share the gospel with those who need to hear it—and who presumably would not come to church absent video screens, concert-hall sound systems, or wacky children's sets complete with slime machines and fire truck baptisteries. The results of these efforts may look good at first, with some churches boasting increased attendance. The data, however, demonstrate otherwise. Alvin Reid, professor of evangelism at Southeastern Baptist Theological Seminary writes,

> Over the preceding twenty years the number of full-time youth pastors had grown dramatically and a plethora of magazines, music, and ideas aimed at youth has been birthed along the way. Meanwhile, during that same time span, the numbers of young people won to Christ dropped at about as fast a rate.[3]

The lesson here is that the church's emphasis on attracting the unchurched through entertainment and child-centered programs has not only not helped, it has hurt. Another researcher concurs, "Sugarcoated Christianity, popular in the 1980s and early 90s, has caused growing numbers of kids to turn away not just from attending youth-fellowship activities but also from practicing their faith at all."[4]

So while the church and parents alike want to raise up spiritual champions, the discipleship model in which church professionals essentially replace parents as the primary agents of discipleship is just not working. One key reason for this was revealed by a comprehensive study on the religious and spiritual lives of American teenagers, which concluded,

> When it comes to the formation of the lives of youth, viewed sociologically, faith communities typically get a very small seat at the end of the table for a very limited period of time.... Religious communities that are interested in the faith formation of their youth simply must better address the structural competition of other, not always supportive institutions and activities. This will likely require developing new and creative norms, practices, and institutions appropriate to specific religious situations and traditions.[5]

That is, the Church must change course. For one thing, we must recognize that a few hours a week of consumer-oriented church events cannot successfully compete for the hearts of young people if those hearts are not being attended to spiritually in the home. The spiritual futures of children must be placed as a matter of primary importance back into the hands of the people who have the greatest opportunity to influence them for the Kingdom of God — their parents.

The idea that fathers and mothers should be the primary agents of discipleship in the lives of their children is hardly a "new and creative norm." It is a scriptural and historical norm. "Fathers, do not provoke your children to anger, but bring them up in the discipline and instruction of the Lord" (Ephesians 6:4). In the Book of Psalms the author writes, "He established a testimony in Jacob and appointed a law in Israel, which he commanded our fathers to teach to their children" (Psalms 78:5). Richard Baxter, the Puritan pastor famous for his disciplined watch over the flock placed in his care, wrote in his classic work to pastors, "Get masters of families to do their duty, and they will not only spare you a great deal of labour, but will much further the success of your labours."[6] What Richard Baxter wrote in 1656 can and should serve as an important paradigm shift for many churches today. Fathers and mothers must be equipped to fulfill their scriptural duty, partnering with the local church to disciple a new generation of faithful and devoted followers of Christ.

It is my desire that this book will help the local church equip parents to engage in the discipleship task. If you are a parent, I am writing this book for you in the hopes that your children, and your children's children, might be afforded the same experience I had as a child—to grow up in a home that loves the Lord and his gospel and demonstrates that love practically, overtly, and consistently. My childhood home was not perfect. Neither is the home I lead, nor any home I know of or have ever heard of. How good it is to know that perfection is not necessary—simply a desire, a plan, prayer, and a regular reliance on God to equip us with the grace and strength to be faithful.

The scriptural and historical record combines with the current research to show that the Church must return to the basics. The Church must again turn its attention to parents, equipping them to both disciple their children and to model for them how to reach other families with the gospel of Jesus Christ.

Now Make It Stick:

1. Take a moment to reflect on your exposure to the gospel as a child. In what ways, if any, did this gospel exposure help you come to faith in Christ?

2. In what ways does your family function as a "little church"?

We pray together as a family:
daily | weekly | monthly | rarely/never
We read the Bible together as a family:
daily | weekly | monthly | rarely/never
We talk about spiritual matters as a family:
daily | weekly | monthly | rarely/never
We share the gospel with others as a family:
daily | weekly | monthly | rarely/never

3. Read Ephesians 6:1-4 and Psalms 78:1-8 and describe in your own words your scriptural responsibility to disciple your children.

Two
THE MIRROR

See

When I was a child, I spoke like a child, I thought like a child, I reasoned like a child. When I became a man, I gave up childish ways. For now we see in a mirror dimly, but then face to face. Now I know in part; then I shall know fully, even as I have been fully known. So now faith, hope, and love abide, these three; but the greatest of these is love. (1 Corinthians 13:11-13)

On the wall in our master bedroom hangs a full-length mirror. Of all the places in the house, it never occurred to me that this spot would be so frequently occupied. At least, not until I connected two salient facts—it is the only full-length mirror in our home, and we have a seven-year-old daughter.

Abby likes fashion. How much of this may be genetic I just don't know, but I am certain her obsession with clothes and accessories has been fostered by her two grandmothers, both of whom are certified professional shoppers. Abby has more outfits than a seven-year-old really needs, and as she studies her stylishness in that bedroom mirror, it seems to me that all she can see is perfection.

Children like the mirror. Me, not so much. I noticed this morning that I am getting more and more gray hair. My physique is not like it was in my "playing" days, and honestly I'm glad I met my wife fourteen years ago and not today. What I see in the mirror is decay; imperfection on the march.

Paul writes something in 1 Corinthians 13:11-13 that will serve us greatly as we begin our family discipleship design project. He alludes to the fact that maturity brings with it the realization that we don't have it all together, that we don't understand everything perfectly. He says, "We see in a mirror dimly," and "We know in part." I find it intriguing that he makes this statement after a passage about giving up childish ways of thinking and reasoning. It is as if Paul is saying, "When I was child, I thought I knew everything and saw myself for who I really was, but now I have left that foolishness behind and recognize I am not as put together as I imagined."

Seeing our own imperfection and vulnerability is vital to the process of family discipleship. That is why we begin our design project with the mirror of Scripture. Like a mirror, the Bible exposes us and tells us the truth about ourselves. As you read through this book you will be confronted with how often you fall short of God's design for discipleship in the home. Trust me—while writing these chapters I was more than once forced to the floor by the Holy Spirit in repentance for my failings as a father, husband, and pastor. So please be encouraged that not one parent who reads this book will honestly be able to approach the content like my daughter approaches that mirror in our bedroom. All of us will be confronted with our flaws and failures. This is the indispensable starting point, the place where hope begins.

Paul writes in I Corinthians 13:12b, "Now I know in part; then I will know fully, even as I have been fully known." As you read, treasure up these words in your heart: "even as I have been fully known." This is such an amazing statement of the grace of God. Although we can only know him and understand him in part, he has known us fully and completely. He knows all of our blind spots, struggles, and fears. He knows our laziness, arrogance, and pride. He knows every point of failure in our lives, and he knew all of these things before he laid the foundation of the world. He knew us fully before he died as our substitute! He knows us today, and makes his grace available to bind up every wound.

Discipleship by Love

A few weeks ago I sat across from a dear friend telling

him a little about this book project. All his children
are young and I know his heart is to see them follow
after Christ. He told me how much he needed this
kind of help because he had no clue where to start in
leading his family spiritually. I have written this book
for him, and for so many parents just like him who
desire with all their hearts to disciple their children,
but no one has ever shown them how. I have written
this book for me, so that I might be able to disciple
my own children and equip the parents in my local
church to do the same. The aim of this book is love.
Love for my children, love for my church, and love
for the body of Christ.

Paul concluded 1 Corinthians 13 with these
words, "So now faith, hope, and love abide, these
three; but the greatest of these is love." The reason
we ought to pursue family discipleship is love! Love
for our children, no matter what age they may be.
I will tell you right now that if you have teenagers
and this is the first time you have considered family
discipleship, the material in this book is going to be
very challenging for you. True discipleship is a long,
steady process, and you have fewer of those especially formative years left to work with. But please
do not be driven away by guilt or fear. Don't doubt
for a moment that God still desires to work through
you in powerful ways for the good of your children.
Be motivated by love to capture the years that

remain for Christ. Remember that our Lord Jesus is able to do "far more abundantly than all that we ask or think, according to the power at work within us" (Ephesians 3:20).

Look in the mirror with me. Let's gaze for a moment at all of our flaws and imperfections, and admit them freely to ourselves. Then let's put down this book, get on our knees, and thank the Lord that despite all of our ugliness, he has redeemed us. He died in our place and for our sin on the cross, even while we were sinners. Let us thank the Lord for our salvation and ask him to do a work in our homes for his glory. The Sovereign King of heaven and earth has the power to transform your home. Let's get started.

Now Make It Stick:

1. Get alone with God and ask him to search your heart, exposing areas of weakness pertaining to parenting and family discipleship. List your failings, and bring these items to Jesus in repentance.
2. Share your list with your spouse and spend time in prayer together, asking the Lord to transform your home for his glory.
3. Set aside an extended period of time to discuss the spiritual condition of each of your children.

4. Write down some specific areas where your children need to grow and develop spiritually, and begin praying together over these items.

Three
THE KITCHEN

The Ingredients of Family Discipleship

He established a testimony in Jacob and appointed a law in Israel, which he commanded our fathers to teach to their children, that the next generation might know them, the children yet unborn, and arise and tell them to their children, so that they should set their hope in God and not forget the works of God, but keep his commandments. (Psalms 78:5-7)

Almost every evening around ten o'clock, I am drawn downstairs from the family room to our kitchen with a gnawing craving for a peanut butter and jelly sandwich. This is one of my favorite moments of the day. Waiting there in the pantry, simply for my indulgence, is a homemade loaf of bread, a jar of peanut butter, a little bear-shaped squeeze-bottle full of honey, and a bag of potato chips. The other necessities await me in the fridge: an ice-cold carton of milk and cherry jelly. Most evenings this ritual plays out perfectly, except for those rare, sad times when some key ingredient is missing. I can live without the chips or the honey, but every so often there is no milk, or we are low on peanut butter, and my hopes for the perfect PB&J vanish.

Some ingredients are simply necessary. This is one reason why I find cooking shows to be an exercise in frustration. When these chef-gurus prance out into their professional kitchens—the kind missing the one wall where the TV cameras go—all the latest high-end culinary equipment is at their disposal. They know things about preparing food that we mortals cannot grasp. Worst of all, they regularly cook with ingredients that have never once been on any shelf in my local supermarket. What is the point of showing people how to cook with ingredients they don't have? Without the right ingredients, everyone knows that a recipe is useless.

Maybe you feel a similar frustration when you hear a pastor announce that it is primarily your responsibility to disciple your children. Perhaps you have inventoried your spiritual pantry of biblical knowledge and, if you are honest, it is not as well-stocked as it needs to be. You know you need ready access to fresh, useful spiritual ingredients if your children are to become, as the psalmist wrote, men and women who set their hope in God. But you're not quite sure what those ingredients are, where to get them, or how to prepare them.

In this chapter, we're going to the supermarket—

a really nice one. It's a supermarket of biblical truth. As we stroll the aisles and review the wares, you are probably going to feel overwhelmed. There is so much your children need to be taught! That's OK. Embrace that feeling. Your sense of helplessness will push you to rely on the grace of God as you take the exciting journey of family discipleship.

Perhaps your children are not exactly children anymore. If so, remember that your call to family discipleship only ends when you die. You have a lifetime to cultivate truth in the hearts of your children. Even when they are adults with their own families, you should lovingly and prayerfully encourage your children in their walk with Jesus. The nature of the parental role changes as our children mature, but its essence does not, and we are called to steward faithfully all the days the Lord has entrusted to us.

As we walk through the supermarket of biblical content, I want to show you seven "aisles" — seven categories — of biblical truth. Thinking in categories helps us to understand and teach God's Word clearly. Imagine a supermarket that stocked its shelves randomly. Trying to find a particular item in aisle after aisle of jumbled chaos would be a nightmare. In a similar way, approaching the Bible without appropriate categories will often produce a certain bewilderment. But categories help us think and teach far more effectively.

Theologians have worked for centuries to compile the biblical data into accessible categories. The seven key categories we will review in this chapter are:

- The Gospel
- The Big Story (Biblical Theology)
- The Big Truths (Systematic Theology)
- The Great Commission
- Spiritual Disciplines
- Christian Living
- Worldview

I'm not saying I plan to teach you all this material in this book. Again, my purpose is here is simply to identify for you the right ingredients. If you will commit to learn from each of these seven categories, you will have all the right ingredients at your fingertips for a lifetime of learning and teaching.

The Gospel

For me, ministering to my children at bedtime is one of the most enjoyable aspects of fatherhood. I treasure the moments I am able to talk with my kids about their day, tell Bible stories, pray over them, and often times sing them to sleep. After all, they are the only people on the planet who want me to sing to them. One of my favorite songs to sing is "The Gospel Song."[7] The beautifully simple and powerful lyrics go like this:

Holy God in love became
Perfect man to bear my blame
On the cross He took my sin
By His death I live again

There is nothing quite so sweet as singing the gospel over my children. One evening, after having sung this chorus multiple times to my three-year-old son, Josiah, I began to hear his little voice singing with me. As tears welled up in my eyes, I silently cried out to God, asking that the gospel truths in this song would plant seeds of grace in my little boy's heart.

The gospel is the most important category of truth for you to stock in your spiritual pantry. If you will commit to nothing else, resolve in your heart today that you will do whatever it takes to saturate your home life with the message of the gospel! Of course, in order to make this commitment you must have a firm grasp on the message yourself.

This is not always easy. There is a great deal of confusion in evangelical culture about the actual content of the biblical gospel. There are even a number of false gospels that are quite prominently practiced and preached. Four in particular are so common that they are openly taught each week in thousands of churches attended by sincere, well-meaning Christians—many of whom can quickly become confused, misguided Christians without ever knowing it. Before we proceed to the true, biblical gospel, let's get these four errors out of the way.

The False Gospel of Personal Improvement

In many circles today the gospel is presented as a means to achieve a better you; your best life now. The gospel of personal improvement urges you to adjust your thinking, attitudes, and actions in order to earn the favor and blessing of God. After all, once you're doing it all right, how could God ignore such an awesome person as you?

The false gospel of personal improvement is nothing more than self-help psychology couched in biblical terminology, with a few scriptural proof-texts ripped from their proper context to try to mask the raging humanism of the message. But God's favor and blessing cannot be earned, purchased, or leveraged. The Bible does not teach that I can become so good that God has to bless me. It teaches that I am so bad that God must either condemn and reject me or forgive and redeem me.

The False Gospel of Prosperity

Did you know that God wants you to be lavishly wealthy? That the Son of God came to earth so that you could buy a new luxury car every two years, own at least one vacation home, and retire early? As ridiculous as it may sound, many people actually believe this. The hope of the prosperity gospel is found in a present-day emphasis on material wealth. I actually heard a prosperity teacher say that the blood of Christ, dripping to the ground as the result of the crown of thorns being jammed onto his head, planted "seeds of prosperity" that are available to every follower of Christ. To appropriate these rich seeds of prosperity, one must simply sow a monetary "seed of faith" to this particular ministry.

Some applications of this view are heretical. All are deeply misguided. The prosperity gospel violates the clear call of Jesus to abandon all to follow him. And for many it is irresistibly appealing.

The False Gospel of Peace and Purpose

The problems with this teaching are less obvious but just as serious. The message is that God's wonderful plan for your life is to give you peace and purpose. Sounds kind of biblical, doesn't it? After all, there is certainly purpose and peace to be found in Christ. But are these two elements a fair and representative summary of the message of the gospel? Did Peter, on the day of Pentecost, proclaim, "Follow Christ, he has a wonderful plan for your life?" No, Peter proclaimed a gospel of deliverance from sin found only in repentance and faith.

In fact, Jesus presents a gospel that from a worldly perspective sounds anything but peaceful.

Do not think that I have come to bring peace to the earth. I have not come to bring peace, but a sword. For I have come to set a man against his father, and a daughter against her mother, and a daughter-in-law against her mother-in-law. And a person's enemies will be those of his own household. Whoever loves father or mother more than me is not worthy of me, and whoever loves son or daughter more than me is not worthy of me. (Matthew 10:34-37)

I recently had the privilege of getting to know a teenage girl, an exchange student from Germany who spent a year with a family in our church. When she arrived, she was staunchly atheistic, as this was her family background. By the grace of God, she was brought to saving faith in Christ during her time with us. Although she rejoiced in her new life, it was very hard for her to go back home and tell her atheistic parents that she is now a follower of Jesus. She has found true spiritual peace, but her decision to follow Christ has brought great relational turmoil.

This is the reality of the gospel; there is no way to make it more palatable or less mysterious to the human mind. The message of the cross will forever be foolishness to those who are perishing, and we should not attempt to make it anything less. If we do, we strip it of its power.

The "Pray the Prayer" False Gospel

This is the granddaddy error of them all. If you have spent much time presenting the gospel to strangers you have probably heard, "I haven't been to church in years, but I am a Christian—when I was in the fifth grade I prayed and asked Jesus into my heart."

Countless people have been taught, explicitly or implicitly, that saying a particular prayer grants them guaranteed entrance into the celestial city. For parents, this is an especially dangerous trap. We naturally want some tangible marker, a way to know that our child is in or out, converted or unconverted. The problem is that no decision a child makes, and no prayer anyone could ever pray, obligates God to forgive anyone of their sins. In response to Nicodemus, Jesus said, "Truly, truly, I say to you, unless one is born again he cannot see the kingdom of God. That which is born of the flesh is flesh, and that which is born of the Spirit is spirit" (John 3:3,6). In John 1:12-13, we read, "But to all who did receive [Jesus], who believed in his name, *he gave the right to become children of God. Who were born, not of blood nor of the will of the flesh nor of the will of man*, but of God."

Salvation is never the result of human choice. It is completely due to the sovereign grace of God working through the proclamation of the gospel. Our decision to follow Christ in repentance and faith comes into play *after* our hearts have been transformed by the gospel message itself; this is why it is so important for us to get the gospel right and to saturate our homes with its message. Scripture teaches us that faith comes by hearing the gospel—the power of God for salvation to those who believe. By this, we know that the most loving act a parent can do for his child is to teach a biblical gospel in the home.

The True Gospel

The good news of Jesus Christ is not that you can become a better person. Or that God has given us the secret to wealth, purpose, and a peaceful life. Or that some special prayer is the "open sesame" for the gates of heaven. The biblical gospel can be understood by keeping in mind four essential elements that summarize its content:

- God is the sovereign and holy Creator of the universe.
- Man has rejected the sovereign and holy rule of God.
- Jesus is the eternal Son of God who came to rescue sinners.
- The gospel demands that all people respond in repentance and faith.

God is the sovereign and holy Creator of the universe. It is vital that our children understand that the gospel belongs to God. He is the King of the universe who created everything for his own glory.

Simply put, God is in control. Sovereignty is a big word that expresses God's supremacy, kingship, and deity. His sovereignty declares him to be God, the incomprehensible Trinity.

God is not only in control, he is also holy. Holiness is most commonly associated with moral purity or perfection, and rightly so, but God's holiness also includes his transcendence. This is critical. God must not be reduced in our estimation to a superior version of ourselves. God is so much greater than us and so different that if we saw him in even a tiny fraction of his glory we would immediately die. It is because of this transcendent otherness that no one can come to know God on their own terms. God alone sets the rules for how we relate to him. In order to know him at all, we must come under his authority.

The truth of God's sovereignty and holiness compels us to reject all so-called gospels that are man-centered. Salvation does not belong to us, but to the Lord (Psalms 3:8; Jonah 4:9; Revelation 7:10). The gospel must always be taught as a God-centered message. The good news is not that we should do something, but rather that God has already accomplished salvation for all who will repent and believe. This is why Paul begins his letter to the Ephesians,

> Blessed be the God and Father of our Lord Jesus Christ, who has blessed us in Christ with every

spiritual blessing in the heavenly places, even as he chose us in him before the foundation of the world, that we should be holy and blameless before him. (Ephesians 1:3-4)

Man has rejected the sovereign and holy rule of God. The Bible clearly teaches, and our experience in life confirms, that we all have sinned and fall short of the glory of God. Each of us, including our children, is born Sons of Adam and Daughters of Eve, sinners by nature to the very core of our being. It is because of our sin, the Bible says, that we are by nature children of wrath, deserving of an eternity separated from the grace and glory of God, experiencing only the fury of his divine justice against our sin. We all are in need of divine rescue. We all need a hero, someone with supernatural power and authority to deliver us from our sin.

Jesus is the eternal Son of God who came to rescue sinners. I treasure the words of the Apostle Paul to Timothy, "The saying is trustworthy and deserving of full acceptance, that Christ Jesus came into the world to save sinners, of whom I am the foremost" (1 Timothy 1:15). What great news! Jesus Christ came into the world to rescue sinners from their sin. Jordan Kauflin of Sovereign Grace Music expresses this truth powerfully when he writes:

I once was lost in darkest night
Yet thought I knew the way
The sin that promised joy and life
Had led me to the grave
I had no hope that You would own
A rebel to Your will
And if You had not loved me first
I would refuse You still

But as I ran my hell-bound race
Indifferent to the cost
You looked upon my helpless state
And led me to the cross
And I beheld God's love displayed
You suffered in my place
You bore the wrath reserved for me
Now all I know is grace

Hallelujah! All I have is Christ
Hallelujah! Jesus is my life

How does Jesus rescue us from our sin? He
came to us not only as a man, but as the God-Man.
He was the image of the invisible God. In Christ, the
world beheld the God of the universe in human flesh
as God the Son stooped down to us, endured every
temptation that we endure, and yet never sinned.
Jesus lived up to God's righteous standard and in

doing so could die on the cross as our representative, in our place and for our sin. In other words, he became our substitute. He took the wrath of God upon himself for us when he died upon the cross. And not only did he die for us, he sealed our rescue when God raised him from the dead.

You see, Jesus did not only make our rescue *possible*, he made our rescue *certain*. If you have left your sin to follow Christ, trusting in him alone to pay the penalty of your sin, the Scripture teaches that Christ died for you on the cross in particular. Many people believe that Christ died for the possibility that some may be saved, but the biblical gospel teaches that Christ died to secure salvation for a particular people. This is why John can write in Revelation concerning Jesus, "Worthy are you to take the scroll and to open its seals, for you were slain, and by your blood you ransomed people for God from every tribe and language and people and nation, and you have made them a kingdom of priests to our God, and they shall reign upon the earth" (Revelation 5:9-10).

The gospel demands that all people respond in repentance and faith. The last element of the gospel is the call to respond in repentance and faith. Repentance simply means to leave your sin, self-rule, and self-sufficiency to follow after Jesus, to accept his rule, and to trust in him completely to forgive your sins. Faith is a gift from God that enables us to believe in the message of the gospel. Mark Dever sums up the gospel nicely in his book, *The Gospel and Personal Evangelism*:

> The good news is that the one and only God, who is holy, made us in his image to know him. But we sinned and cut ourselves off from him. In his great love, God became a man in Jesus, lived a perfect life, and died on the cross, thus fulfilling the law himself and taking on himself the punishment for the sins of all those who would ever turn and trust in him. He rose again from the dead, showing that God accepted Christ's sacrifice and that God's wrath against us had been exhausted. He now calls us to repent of our sins and to trust in Christ alone for our forgiveness. If we repent of our sins and trust in Christ, we are born again into a new life, an eternal life with God.[9]

We have lingered long in the Gospel aisle, and for the best of reasons. We must not miss the centrality of the gospel to family discipleship. Without it we cannot expect our children to know the Lord or persevere in their faith.

The Big Story

The entire Bible is one glorious account of God's work to redeem for himself a people, for his own possession, who will one day inhabit a restored paradise. The Bible is the story of God reconciling a people and the entire universe to himself. This is what we find in Aisle 2. I call this category The Big Story. Theologians call it Biblical Theology.

The Big Story Points to God

If your childhood church experience was anything like mine, then perhaps you too were victimized by the travesty of quarterly Sunday School literature. I'm thinking particularly of the endless parade of topical morality tales drawn from the historical figures and events of Scripture and packaged into weekly lessons. When this approach represents the core of a child's Bible education, he never learns the most important story line ever composed. He never learns The Big Story.

Consider the account of Joseph from the book of Genesis. Often this wonderful story appears in Sunday School as a character sketch. Joseph is presented as a model of perseverance, patience, hard work, and self-control, such a great guy that God elevates him from being a prisoner to being the second most powerful ruler in the known world.

But this view ignores the reason why God chose

to preserve the story in the first place. Joseph himself tells us the purpose of his life story when he talks to his brothers about how they sold him into slavery: "As for you, you meant it evil against me, but God meant it for good, to bring it about that many people should be kept alive, as they are today" (Genesis 50:20). Joseph understood clearly, although somewhat generally, why he went through all those lows and highs. As the Bible unfolds we see the reason more specifically—it was because of the sovereign plan of God to preserve for himself a people and place them in Egypt so that he would one day rescue them from the bondage of slavery as a picture of his perfect and final redeeming work in Christ. Unless you study Joseph in light of The Big Story, this truth disappears.

The Bible is not *about* how Joseph was honorable, or how young David was brave, or how Mary was full of faith, as true as those things are. The Bible is *about* God working in the lives of men, women, and children, directing all of history toward a sure conclusion. God is the main character of Scripture and his sovereign grace is vividly on display, from Genesis to Revelation.

Reading the Bible to extract its "life lessons" puts much of the focus on the *reader* of Scripture. But the real story of the Bible is about the Author. The Big Story will help you replace the Bible's mystery with wonder. As you come to understand that story, you discover God's plan of redemption running through every page of Scripture. Where once you saw morality tales, you now see a further unfolding of the character of God. God becomes the key figure, his majesty displayed in each and every event.

The Big Story Constructively Reformulates the Hard Questions

Another key advantage of Biblical Theology is that it gives us a means to deal with the difficult *passages* in the Bible by relating them to the one *message* of the Bible. Some passages in the Old Testament, for example, such as those where God requires the Israelites to destroy the people of Canaan, can seem cold and harsh. In reaction, some professing Christians today simply reject the God of the Old Testament in favor of the New Testament God. The problem with this method is that we have no right to decide what God—who is the same yesterday, today, and forever—can or cannot do.

It's perfectly fine to ask, "How could God have required the Israelites to kill all those people?" The problem emerges when we try to answer such questions without remembering that the Bible was given to teach us about the character and purposes of God—not to reinforce our personal opinions about who God ought to be. The Bible is a gift from God intended in large part to teach us what do not yet know, or do not yet know well enough. It is *supposed* to challenge us.

When we see that the Bible is really telling one Big Story about God and his purposes, we can come to difficult or challenging passages with a far more constructive approach. We can ask, "What does this passage teach us from the perspective of the entire story of the Bible?"

In Reformulating Hard Questions, the Big Story Leads to the Gospel

Let's stick with that question about the Canaanites. In the Bible's story line, God chose to allow his glory to reside in Israel as an act of grace, and he gave the Israelites specific laws and customs to ensure that they related to him properly. Canaan is a typology of the future and perfect Promised Land that will culminate in the creation of a new heaven and earth completely free of sin. But the Canaanites who dwelt in the land prior to the arrival of the Israelites were an idolatrous and rebellious people. God's glory could never reside in a land where such rampant evil was practiced. The Canaanites had to be removed. The Promised Land had to be cleansed.

Real people died when the Canaanites were slaughtered. It was a tragedy. In fact, ever since Adam and Eve sinned, humanity has been living in a tragedy, with every death and every tear and every sad and unhappy and painful event pointing to the awfulness of sin and rebellion. The Big Story is that God is *redeeming* that tragedy in the only way that is in keeping with his holiness and his will. The story of the Canaanites is a shocking, graphic, gruesome reminder—not of a capricious God with a grudge against a particular people—but of how seriously God takes this matter of holiness. To God, even the typology of holiness is deadly serious stuff.

God told Israel to put the Canaanites to death because in eternity there will be no more sin. And there will be no more sin because the Son of God was himself put to death, so that death itself might be defeated. Because of Christ's death, every believer will worship before the throne, cleansed by the blood of the Lamb and clothed in the perfect righteousness of Jesus. We will relate to God perfectly, not because we deserve to behold his glory, but only due to the perfect sacrifice of Jesus. The cleansing of Canaan will pale in comparison to God's judgment of those who die in their sin.

This is how the Big Story changes the nature of the questions we ask about Scripture, and this is how it leads us to the gospel. Biblical Theology—the Big Story—helps us relate all of Scripture to the person and work of Jesus Christ and the message of the gospel. In Luke 24:25-32, Jesus himself used the Bible in this way on the road to Emmaus.

"O foolish ones, and slow of heart to believe all that the prophets have spoken! Was it not necessary that the Christ should suffer these things and enter into his glory?" And beginning with Moses and all the Prophets, he interpreted to them in all the Scriptures the things concerning himself. So they drew near to the village to which they were going. He acted as if he were going farther, but they urged him strongly, saying, "Stay with us, for it is toward evening and the day is now far spent." So he went in to stay with them. When he was at table with them, he took the bread and blessed and broke it and gave it to them. And their eyes were opened, and they recognized him. And he vanished from their sight. They said to each other, "Did not our hearts burn within us while he talked to us on the road, while he opened to us the Scriptures?"

What an amazing encouragement to study Biblical Theology. Jesus himself understood how all of Scripture relates to himself. We must also endeavor to help our children see how all of Scripture points us to Christ, demonstrating the continuity between law and grace and removing the idea that somehow God changed (or changed course) between the Old Testament and the New.

The Big Truths

Aisle 3 of our supermarket of biblical truth contains what theologians call Systematic Theology. This is an effort to compile everything the Scripture says about a particular topic and systemize the results into statements of doctrinal truth. Theologians have broken down the teaching of the Bible into several big categories of truth. These are Big Truths indeed: God's Word; God's Character; The Trinity; Creation and God's Providential Rule; Human Nature and Sin; The Person of Jesus; The Work and Ministry of Jesus; The Person and Work of the Holy Spirit; Salvation; The Church; and Last Things.

Many Christians shy away from theological learning and study. They think it's too hard, or not important, or even unspiritual (the authors of Scripture would disagree!). This is a huge mistake. Your children are going to formulate their ideas about the Bible, God, man, and salvation from *somewhere*. If you do not teach your children biblical doctrine, they will be forced to synthesize key ideas (about who God is and who they are) from random bits of truth and falsehood they collect from church, peers, teachers, and the media.

In 2 Kings 22, Hilkiah the High Priest discovers the book of the law in the temple while gathering money for temple renovations. Think about that. The *High Priest*, while busying himself about *fund-*

raising, stumbles on the Word of God and at first he isn't quite sure what it is! It had been gathering dust for seventy-five years, and those charged with overseeing the spiritual health of God's people hadn't bothered to look for it for *decades*! King Josiah, to his credit, realizes he probably ought to know what it says. When it is read aloud to him, he weeps and rips his clothes and cries out,

> Go, inquire of the LORD for me, and for the people, and for all Judah, concerning the words of this book that has been found. For great is the wrath of the LORD that has been kindled against us, because our fathers have not obeyed the words of this book, to do according to all that is written concerning us. (2 Kings 22:13)

The people of Judah had been ignorant of the Word of God for two generations and as a result were suffering terribly. King Josiah brought the people back to God's Word, and went on to become one of Judah's greatest kings. The nation flourished under his rule.

Knowing and teaching the Big Truths of Scripture to our children is vital to their spiritual growth and development. I pray that our homes will discover the Big Truths about God from the Bible. I pray that the Big Truths will not remain buried in our homes for generations. May the Big Truths transform our homes as they transformed Josiah and the nation of Judah.

The Great Commission

The Bible not only teaches us what we ought to believe about God. It shows us that God has a purpose for his people in this earth, what that purpose is, and how he desires to use us to help accomplish it. God has given his people the great task of taking his gospel into the world. It is vital that our children see the missional heart of God for the world, while coming to understand how God is glorified through our faithful witness. That's the aisle we're in now.

One of my favorite Bible passages is 2 Corinthians 4:4-7.

In their case the god of this world has blinded the minds of the unbelievers, to keep them from seeing the light of the gospel of the glory of Christ, who is the image of God. For what we proclaim is not ourselves, but Jesus Christ as Lord, with ourselves as your servants for Jesus' sake. For God, who said, "Let light shine out of darkness," has shone in our hearts to give the light of the knowledge of the glory of God in the face of Jesus Christ. But we have this treasure in jars of clay, to show that the surpassing power belongs to God and not to us.

Here we see that in the gospel we are given the great treasure of the "knowledge of the glory of God in the face of Jesus Christ." This treasure is not given to us because we are worthy vessels. Rather, we are plain old everyday jars of clay, easily broken and not very interesting or attractive. God has not given us Christ so that people will make much of us; he has given us Christ so that we will make much of him!

I recently heard of some folks who left a local church because it had "adopted" a Muslim people group as a particular focus of prayer and evangelism. They left the church because they thought that bringing the gospel to Muslims was anti-Semitic. These precious people were misguided about the missional heart of God. Somehow they had seriously missed the point!

How vital it is that our children understand the heart of God for the nations. Our eternity is in heaven, but God keeps us on this earth for a purpose! Revelation 5 demonstrates the beauty of God's redemptive purpose in saving people from every tribe, tongue, and people. Our children must come to love the nations with God's heart for their salvation.

And not just the nations, but also our neighbors. I remember as a child watching my dad walk across the street many evenings right after he pulled in the driveway. Our neighbor was often in his garage tinkering with his car. I didn't think very deeply about the small moments Dad spent across the street until the Sunday morning that man and his wife came to our church and professed faith in Christ. Then it hit me; Dad hadn't just been shooting the breeze. He had been building a relationship with that man, and at opportune moments speaking of the powerful, life-changing gospel of Jesus Christ.

Christians often refer to Matthew 28:18-20 as the Great Commission. I think we should rename it the Great Privilege. What an extraordinary honor it is to have this as our calling! Let us teach and model for our children the tremendous joy and honor of helping to share Jesus with those who do not know him, whether those unsaved live across the street or across the ocean.

Spiritual Disciplines

While this is a short section of the book, the aisle it represents is as long as life itself, for the spiritual disciplines are an essential means of spiritual growth. Paul wrote to Timothy, "Train yourself for godliness" (1 Timothy 4:7b). Training involves discipline. The plain truth is that many parents teach children to be disciplined students and disciplined athletes, but when it comes to *spiritual* disciplines, the expectations are far lower and the emphasis greatly reduced.

Donald Whitney, in his book *Spiritual Disciplines for the Christian Life*, outlines five basic disciplines: Bible intake, prayer, worship, service, and stewardship.[10] It is critical that you teach your children the basic disciplines of the Christian life and their roots in Scripture, and then help them form habits that will serve them their entire lives. After all, "while bodily training is of some value, godliness is of value in every way, as it holds promise for the present life and also for the life to come" (1 Timothy 4:8).

Christian Living

By now you may be growing weary of all these aisles. That's not unusual for a trip to the supermarket, but the good news is that we only have two more aisles to explore.

In the Christian Living aisle we find a broad category of subjects involving how we actually walk out our faith in daily life. Some of the major subcategories in this aisle are forgiveness, sexual purity, parenting, marriage and family, and making right choices. Most of the time when we talk about "Christian books," we are referring to books that help us honor God in areas like these.

You need to use discernment when selecting books on the Christian life. Each one comes from a particular theological perspective, and if you aren't intentional about identifying what that perspective is, you can be influenced without knowing it. Some very popular material produced by Christians teaches dangerous theological falsehoods, including:

- Open Theism (God does not know the future in detail)
- Universalism (all people will ultimately be saved), or
- Modalism (God is not a Trinity—three persons in one God—but one person who appears in different forms at different times)

I urge you to take the effort to learn sound doctrine so that you can effectively discern the truthfulness of various materials widely available in the Christian marketplace. Of course, there are many solid and helpful books in this category. Just don't judge a book by its cover or its popularity; look for its theological leanings.

Worldview

We are finally here, the last aisle of biblical content—the category of Worldview. Worldview is the lens through which we interpret all that we learn and experience. As a category of truth, worldview helps us think biblically about all of life, so that we can make sense of the world around us and defend the faith based on "the hope that is within you" (1 Peter 3:15).

Music, movies, television, books, video games, websites, and textbooks are all influenced by some way of seeing the world, so the study of worldview is crucial in helping children analyze the cultural information they absorb on a daily basis. A worldview that is not genuinely biblical and therefore God-centered will inevitably be man-centered. But as we pass along to our children a sound Christian worldview, we equip them to navigate the waters of our humanistic, postmodern culture. This may include teaching them how to argue against atheism or scientific naturalism/evolution, and to speak clearly on ethical issues such as abortion, stem cell research, and homosexuality. Worldview also helps us develop biblical philosophies for education, economics, and law. Make sure your own you of this world in which God has placed us is solidly biblical, and then pass it along to your children.

How Do I Start to Prepare Myself?

I warned you—at this point you might feel just a little overwhelmed. There is so much information in the Bible to absorb, so much we are supposed to understand and be reasonably good at in order to be effective parents. You may be tempted to throw in the towel right now. Why not simply trust in God's sovereignty for your children's care? Don't you have enough of a load already? Don't you know people who seem to be doing well as Christians, when they weren't even raised in Christian homes, much less diligent and intentional Christian homes?

Sure, that definitely does happen, for our God

is able to redeem any life. But God did not give your children to a non-Christian home. He brought them into your home, and your care. He gave them to you—and he knows your strengths and weaknesses, all the good and all the bad, far better than you do. Remember the last time you lost your temper with your children? Or all the times you have neglected to love and serve them with consistent biblical instruction? God knew that was coming. Those were some of the sins Christ hung on the cross to forgive. We don't know all the ways in which God works his will, but we do know that he gave you these particular children for your good, for their good, and for his glory.

So let me encourage you to stay the course. One practical way I want to do that is to outline some principles that will help you get on the right track.

This book offers a big-picture understanding of what it means to be an effective and intentional Christian parent. But it is more than a book of theory, for I would do you a great disservice if I were never to suggest any action steps. Family discipleship is ultimately a commitment to be a disciple yourself. You can't teach your children what you don't know. You can't model for your children what you are unwilling to do. You have to count the cost and commit to equip yourself in each of the content areas outlined in this chapter. I recommend that you make some commitments to your own discipleship right now.

First, you must immediately commit to read the Bible from cover to cover in ninety days. Turn off the television set, shut down the computers, put your cell phone in another room, ask for the cooperation of your family members, and dive into the text.

You can do this. It will be a marker for you, the beginning of a new season, and will help reorient your purpose. This will be how you prove to yourself you're actually serious about being an intentional Christian parent. Because I promise you that if you won't commit to read your Bible, you will never commit to family discipleship.

After you read the Bible all the way through, commit to a reading plan that will help you read from every part of Scripture on a regular basis. Pure Bible knowledge is your most important asset in family discipleship.

Second, commit to read one book per year from each of the seven categories. (See the Recommended Reading.) That is only seven books per year, less than one a month. As you finish them, keep them all on a single bookshelf. If you commit to this task, in a few short years you will develop a nice discipleship library. In just ten short years you will own more than seventy carefully selected volumes across the spectrum of biblical topics. This will serve as a huge advantage to you. If you have small children, by the time they are teenagers you will have a wealth of books for them to read on their own. The biggest payoff is the fact that you will be learning continually from every category.

Third, journal or blog what you are learning and discuss it with other Christian parents. Perhaps the best way to do this is to learn along with people whose life situation is similar to yours. Discipleship always works better as a group activity. Your fellow disciples can help hold you accountable in these areas, too. I have been involved in a book-study group for five years, and it has been one of the most enriching discipleship experiences of my life.

Fourth, commit yourself to a church that values expositional preaching and solid theological training. One of the worst mistakes you can make is to join a church for the style of music or the entertainment value of the youth ministries. Commit to a church that will partner with you in family discipleship by faithfully teaching you and your children God's Word.

Finally, recycle what you are learning. Simply begin to share and model at home what you are learning. If a passage of Scripture blesses you during the week, share this with your family! If you came under the conviction of the Spirit during Sunday's message, share this with your family! If you discover a great nugget of truth while reading a good book, share it with your family! If God shows you something you need to do, share it with your family and start doing it! Simply recycle into your home what God is doing in you personally. Don't fall into the trap of growing spiritually while starving your family. It would be like a man eating a huge lunch at work every day while his family lives on rice and beans.

My prayer is that you will embrace the pursuit of knowledge for the glory of Christ. I encourage you to sit down with your spouse and develop a strategy to begin stocking your pantry right away. I promise that you will be blessed in your efforts.

Now Make It Stick:

1. Take inventory of your biblical knowledge by looking at the seven categories discussed in this chapter. A low number indicates little or no knowledge of the topic while a high number indicates the ability to freely and accurately teach and discuss it. Circle one number in each category.

The Gospel

    1   2   3   4   5   6   7   8   9   10

The Big Story (Biblical Theology)

    1   2   3   4   5   6   7   8   9   10

The Big Truths (Systematic Theology)

    1   2   3   4   5   6   7   8   9   10

The Great Commission

    1   2   3   4   5   6   7   8   9   10

Spiritual Disciplines

   1   2   3   4   5   6   7   8   9   10

Christian Living

   1   2   3   4   5   6   7   8   9   10

Worldview

   1   2   3   4   5   6   7   8   9   10

2. What time-killers can you eliminate from your daily schedule that will help you immediately begin to read the entire Bible and finish in 90 days?

3. See the Recommended Reading. Pick one book from each category to read this year.

4. List any opportunities your local church provides to grow in any of the seven categories:

The Gospel:

The Big Story:

The Big Truths:

The Great Commission:

Spiritual Disciplines:

Christian Living:

Worldview:

Four
THE LIVING ROOM

Contexts for Teaching and Learning

Hear, O Israel: The LORD our God, the LORD is one. You shall love the LORD your God with all your heart and with all your soul and with all your might. And these words that I command you today shall be on your heart. You shall teach them diligently to your children, and shall talk of them when you sit in your house, and when you walk by the way, and when you lie down, and when you rise. You shall bind them as a sign on your hand, and they shall be as frontlets between your eyes. You shall write them on the doorposts of your house and on your gates. (Deuteronomy 6:4-9)

So many of my best childhood memories are set in living rooms. In living rooms I watched football with Dad, played cards with Mom, and picked fights with my younger brother. And I will never forget the Christmas morning I found a brand new Atari 2600 hooked up to the television set. For so many families, the living room is a place where life happens, conversations abound, decisions are made, and lessons are learned.

In 1992 I was a 17-year-old junior at Rogers High School in Rogers, Arkansas. We had been living in that town for fifteen years when one evening my father, a Baptist pastor, gathered us all in the living room to share with us his decision to take the pastorate of a church in Fort Smith, Arkansas, about seventy-five miles away. I remember my emotions in that moment. I could sense that Mom and Dad were no more eager to move me to a new city and high school in the middle of my junior year than I was. But there in the living room, as my Dad shared his heart and as we prayed together as a family, I sensed that God was going to do a new work in my life. And that he did. Memories are made and life happens in living rooms.

In the previous chapter we learned how to stock a kitchen with well-organized categories of biblical knowledge. But not one ounce of that knowledge will be useful in family discipleship if we don't understand how and when to share it with our children. Never forget that knowledge is meant to be passed on. The writer of Hebrews challenged his audience by scolding them, saying, "By this time you ought to be teachers" (Hebrews 5:12). I lay this same challenge at your feet. God intends for you to know him and to *make him known*, especially to your children.

Stocking the Kitchen was about content. As we consider the Living Room, our focus shifts to teaching and learning—specifically, the four spheres of family discipleship. Within each sphere, we will learn to recognize and take advantage of the almost constant stream of opportunities we have to pass along the content of Scripture in memorable and life-changing ways. Remember, however, that the Living Room is merely a metaphor. Family discipleship is to take place in every "room" of life. Before we discuss the four spheres of family discipleship I want to take a moment to look at the foremost passage in the Bible that speaks to our topic.

The Biblical Methodology of Family Discipleship

The book of Deuteronomy offers us wonderful instruction for implementing family discipleship. The book contains the last three speeches Moses made to Israel as they stood at the edge of the Jordan River before entering the Promised Land. An entire rebellious generation had died in the wilderness of Kadesh, and Moses himself was now forbidden from entering the Land. This, then, was Moses' last opportunity to speak to God's covenant people. He took the occasion to restate the Law of God and the covenantal responsibilities of the people to hear and obey it. In Deuteronomy Chapter 6, Moses calls

Israel to love and obey the one true God, and challenges the people to integrate God's Word seamlessly into every aspect of their lives, so that it becomes the very foundation of their families and community.

Inherent in this passage is the idea that God's people are a people of his revealed Word. We have been called to hear the Word of God and, in Deuteronomy 6:1, we are commanded to internalize this word in our hearts. The law of God is never taught effectively unless it has first transformed the character of the teacher. Moses tells the people that these words must be *on their hearts* and then they must teach them to their children.

Eugene Merrill writes, "To be upon the heart is to be in one's constant, conscious reflection."[11] This nuance is a vital one for us as we contemplate actually doing family discipleship. We must be honest about our own level of discipleship. Every one of us must cry out as the Psalmist, "With my whole heart I seek you; let me not wander from your commandments! I have stored up your word in my heart that I might not sin against you" (Psalms 119:10-11).

A simple principle can be derived from this discussion; *you cannot disciple your children beyond your own level of discipleship*. If you are not faithful to meditate on the Scripture daily, you will not be able to train your children to do so. If you do not model a life of intimate prayer, you will not be able to teach your children how to pray. If you never share the gospel outside the home, you will not be able to teach your children how to share the gospel with their friends.

Quite simply, you must make a personal commitment to love God with all your heart and with all your soul—your whole self, including your rationality, mental capacity, moral choices and will, inner feelings and desires, and the deepest roots of your life.[12]

Moses on Intentional Parenting

The Bible's first specific mention of family discipleship appears in Deuteronomy 6:7, "You shall teach them [God's words] diligently to your children, and shall talk of them when you sit in your house, and when you walk by the way, and when you lie down, and when you rise." Here we are confronted with the crucial responsibility of teaching and instructing our children in the Scripture in a way that is both *routine* and *repetitive*. Only by building these practices into our lives as parents can we expect God's Word to become ingrained into the lives of our children.

The phrase translated "teach them diligently" in the ESV, is translated "impress them" in the NIV. Merrill illuminates the idea of impressing the Scripture on our children when he writes:

> The image is that of the engraver of a monument who takes hammer and chisel in hand and

with painstaking care etches a text into the face of a solid slab of granite. The sheer labor of such a task is daunting indeed, but once done the message is there to stay. Thus it is that the generations of Israelites to come must receive and transmit the words of the Lord's everlasting covenant revelation.[13]

This is a wonderful illustration for us as we prepare ourselves for the discipleship task. Etching requires routine, dedication, focus, knowledge, skill, and consistency, as we repeatedly teach God's Word and apply its truths to everyday life.

In Deuteronomy 6:7-9 Moses gets more specific, using the words *talk*, *tie*, *bind*, and *write* to help us understand how important repetition is to this parental task of discipleship. Merrill continues, "In less figurative terms and yet with clear hyperbole, Moses said that the way this message is made indelible is by constant repetition."[14]

Moses is saying, first, that parents need to have as their goal the *complete saturation of God's Word into family and community life* and, second, that this saturation is *necessary* to ensure the generational faithfulness of God's covenant people. The fact is that every day secular culture immerses our children in a particular view of the world. As Christian parents we are called to counteract this by continually teaching and reinforcing the Word of God in our children's hearts and minds. And while God is the one who makes our effort effective, he nevertheless commands us to *make* the effort. In Deuteronomy 6, Moses is saying is that unless we do so, we should not expect positive results in the lives of our children. That is the message of Scripture for parents.

Moses understood that God's truth cannot effectively be taught if it is confined to the home or classroom. How will our children believe that the Bible is about all of life if we only talk about it during the Bible lesson? Deuteronomy 6 reverses that dynamic by transforming all of life into one *ongoing* Bible lesson.

To put it another way, *discipleship is most effectively accomplished when the practice is integrated into the rhythm of everyday life*. A consistent time of family worship, for example, is a great discipleship practice, but it is no substitute for a lifestyle of discipleship that encompasses the breakfast table, the car, bedtime, errands, and chores. There is not a single moment in life that cannot be used as an opportunity for instruction.

Deuteronomy 6 helps us see that God gave his Word to assist us in our efforts to take every thought captive for Christ (2 Corinthians 10:5) and to exercise self-control in all things (Galatians 5:23). It is *through* God's Word that we can *obey* God's Word and thereby love and serve God comprehensively in our personal life, family life, and public life.

The Goal of Parenthood

What is the ultimate purpose and goal in teaching our children the Bible and the application of truth to everyday life? The answer is found in the remaining verses of Deuteronomy 6.

Moses tells the Israelites the LORD is going to give them Canaan in fulfillment of his promises to Abraham, Isaac, and Jacob. He is reminding the Israelites that it is the Lord who is dropping all these good things into their laps.[15] Moses then issues a warning, "Then take care lest you forget the Lord, who brought you out of the land of Egypt, out of the house of slavery" (Deuteronomy 6:12). Moses is letting them know that the goal of all this teaching is not to place them under an oppressive burden of religious duty, but to help them worship God rightly in response to his saving grace. Wright examines this idea when he suggests, "Obedience, though sanctioned by the reality of God's wrath, should primarily be motivated by gratitude and love in response to God's grace."[16]

The ultimate goal of discipleship is that our children will come to delight in the grace of God and desire to love and obey him. They will develop these attitudes only if they understand what God has done for them. If they do not understand the grace of God, then the Bible becomes a rigid, legalistic system. Moses tells the people what to say when their children ask, "What is the meaning of the testimonies and the statutes and the rules?" They are to tell the story of God's gracious and miraculous deliverance of his people from Egypt. They are to tell their children that God's standards are for their good and to command them to be careful to worship and obey God only (Deuteronomy 6:20-25).

For us, then, the teaching task ultimately consists of telling the story of God's faithfulness so that our children will come to worship the one true God in response to his saving grace. We are called to the ongoing proclamation and celebration of the gospel in the hope that our kids will come to know Christ and walk with him all of their days. Please realize that eternity is at stake. We must deliver God's Word to our children in every sphere of life, taking advantage of every opportunity we can to offer our children the wisdom and worldview of Scripture.

The Four Spheres of Family Discipleship

In order to follow God's commands for family discipleship as relayed through Moses, we must have a strategy. How can we constructively incorporate God's Word into the daily routine of family life? To begin with, we must be aware of the four spheres of family discipleship: The Home, The Community, The Church, and The World. In this way we can come to recognize the continual opportunities available to us.

A good friend and elder at my church always encourages me to remember a simple but profound truth, "Pastor," he says, "What gets structured gets done." I want to help you take that advice. At the end of this section, you will have the ability to intentionally plan discipleship opportunities as part of your daily schedule. Because it's true: what gets structured gets done.

Sphere One: The Home

Your home is most likely the first place that comes to mind when you think about instructing your children in the things of God, and for most families it is certainly the most significant place. After all, this is where you wake up and go to sleep, where you eat most of your meals and enjoy most of your family time. Home can and should be a safe place to discuss deep spiritual truths and to ask tough questions about God and his Word.

Let's consider some routine home situations that present opportunities for discipleship.

Mealtimes. From prayer, to conversation, to sharing, to reflection on the day's events or anticipation of events still to come, every meal presents rich opportunities for discipleship.

Failing to pray before a meal is not a sin, but it is a lost opportunity, and family discipleship is all about seizing opportunities. Shared meals provide us with regular occasions to express gratitude to God and model prayerfulness to one another. One danger, of course, is getting into a prayer rut where we speak more from habit than from gratitude.

Every time our son Josiah prays at mealtime, he says, "Dear God, please help us wash our bodies." Why does he do this? Because when I pray before a meal, I usually open with "Dear God" and at some point ask that the food would "nourish our bodies." At age three, Josiah isn't quite sure what *nourish* means so he does the best he can!

Token prayers are the easiest kind to pray, and perhaps the most common. But it is far more instructive and effective to take the time to say a genuine and thoughtful prayer. In even a brief prayer we can offer thanksgiving, glorify God by drawing attention to his attributes, petition him for grace, and more. Let us resist the temptation is to mutter a token prayer— we are speaking to our heavenly Father.

Family breakfast together offers a rich opportunity to start the day from a biblical perspective, praying for one another and encouraging each other in Christlikeness. Dinner time offers a chance to engage in spiritual dialogue about the day, share challenges, and encourage one another with God's faithfulness.

Discipline. Although times of discipline represent one of the greatest discipleship opportunities a parent can have, many Christian parents miss it completely by misunderstanding the purpose of discipline in the first place. Discipline in the home, whether physical or verbal, is not about getting your children to behave in a certain way. Children cannot obey perfectly and they never will. If you discipline your children to condition them to perform certain behaviors, you are not raising them in the fear and admonition of the Lord. You are training them in self-righteousness.

Discipline without biblical instruction, in my opinion, is child abuse. But discipline with biblical instruction is a biblical requirement for parents. The point of such discipline is to instruct a child in his need for a Savior. Appropriate discipline is a demonstration of how God relates to us in our sin. Discipline is the time to help a child better understand the truth about his sin nature and the reality of God's anger and wrath against sin.

Discipline should be consistent, just, and exercised in love. God's anger against our sin is not a wild, capricious, or vengeful anger. It is controlled, intentional, purposeful, and redemptive—and these qualities should mark the discipline of our children.

The practice in my house is to make it a point to share the gospel every time we discipline, especially if corporal punishment is involved. Do not miss the precious opportunities that discipline affords. When we must discipline our children for sinful behavior, we come close to touching the heart of the gospel.

Bedtime. Particularly when children are younger, bedtime represents a unique opportunity for parents. You couldn't ask for a better set of circumstances—a predictable daily window when the day is winding down, distractions are at a minimum, and the world can be pushed back for a moment while you focus all your attention on being alone with and ministering to your child. For me, these times revolve around prayer, conversation, and singing.

Bedtime is my opportunity to pray over my children consistently. This is a little different from simply saying bedtime prayers. It is important for my children to hear me pray *for* them—for spiritual blessing and, if they are still unregenerate, for salvation. In these moments I pour out my heart to God openly so that my kids know exactly what I desire for them spiritually. I pray that God would use them for his glory, that he would help them love Jesus more than anyone or anything else, that they will be blessed with a godly spouse, and many other requests. In addition to God hearing these prayers, I believe that as my children hear these prayers they will be spiritually encouraged and strengthened.

Bedtime also provides unique opportunities

to talk with our children about spiritual truth and perhaps to sing the truth over them. Select songs and hymns that are full of gospel truth, and use repetition so the words can sink down into their hearts.

Bedtime rituals will change as children age, but a wise parent makes it a habit to capture bedtime for discipleship.

Family worship. When you consider family discipleship, your first thought may be of family worship or devotions. In this book I have avoided making that association, because for far too many Christian families, "family worship" has become an easy out. Getting together as a family on a consistent basis for devotions is an excellent thing to do, but it is no substitute for a healthy spiritual life as a family, and no guarantee of it either.

Having said that, setting aside specific times to read the Bible, pray, sing, or have a short devotion as a family can be a truly powerful means of growing together spiritually. If your family does not practice this I strongly encourage you to begin doing so.

First, family worship should prioritize the reading of God's Word. The simplest method of family worship is to read a passage of Scripture together and then talk about the text. The length of the passage and depth of discussion will vary with the ages of your children, but the Word of God is powerful to change hearts and homes.

Second, you can utilize the Sunday sermon as a springboard for discussion and teaching. This is especially effective if your children are with you in the service and are challenged to listen and take notes. This not only reinforces biblical truth, it encourages and amplifies the importance of corporate worship.

There are several family devotional guides and books available to help you in family worship. You may also want to make use of catechisms. Catechisms are an effective means of teaching doctrine by instructing children to memorize or be familiar with various questions and answers relating to a particular truth. To catechize simply means to teach doctrine in an orderly way. There are many solid catechisms available free of charge.

Family worship is also an opportune time to make use of scripturally and theologically rich music. Children typically enjoy singing, so teaching and incorporating songs into family worship is normally an easy task. For parents with teenagers, try delving into the world of theologically rich Christian music. Thankfully, there are many artists today, of a variety of genres, who write challenging and Christ-centered lyrics to music that is relevant to your student's young ears—and you can usually find the words online if your old ears can't quite catch them all.

Ideas for practicing discipleship in the home are endless. Take some time to think intentionally about how to teach biblical truth to your children at home. Go through each day alert for opportunities to pursue family discipleship.

Sphere Two: The Community

The second sphere of family discipleship is the community. We live a large portion of our lives outside of the walls of our home. We learn, play, eat, shop, and work in our community. When thinking about discipleship it is vital not to compartmentalize learning in one or two spheres. Biblical truth applies to all of life and must be taught and modeled in every sphere.

In order to practice discipleship in the community you have to live with your eyes wide open. When you find yourself out in public with your children, don't allow yourself to be so immersed in your to-do list that you pass over important teaching moments. God is moving and working all around us and we often miss opportunities because we are so self-absorbed. How can you live with your eyes wide open for discipleship opportunities? Here are three suggested areas.

Prayer walk/drive. Whenever you are out driving or walking with your children, observe what is going on around you and pray out loud for what God lays on your heart. You will be amazed at all the opportunities to pray and minister in your community when you begin to look at the world through a spiritual lens. Your children will begin to see the world differently as well. People on the sidewalk will become more than just passing shadows. The poor will become more than an inconvenience. Houses will become more than buildings. A whole world of ministry will come alive through prayer.

Imagine for a moment the discipleship potential of weekly prayer walks through your neighborhood with your children. There is no end to the ministry possibilities and opportunities to share the gospel as you pray over the homes and talk with neighbors about their spiritual needs. You might even begin to prayer-walk through the mall and grocery store.

Serve your community. This could involve visiting a local nursing home with your children, helping them start a ministry to widows in your church, or any number of other things. The simple key is to help your children develop the habit of living with their spiritual eyes wide open. This will help them see and love their community with the love of Christ.

One way I have found to serve is by coaching my daughter's community soccer team. A minimal time investment gives me a huge opportunity to invest in my community while affording a strategic opportunity to teach my daughter how to reach out to new friends with the gospel.

Real-time teachable moments. In the book of Acts we see a church that had a massive impact on its community. A key reason is that they did not have the luxury of being able to isolate themselves from the culture at large. By contrast, we have Christian music, movies, magazines, and really cheesy Christian board games. We have basketball, football, soccer and cheerleading in Christian leagues. Many churches have their own basketball courts and workout facilities. As a general rule, the more prosperous the church or the society, the more easily Christians can live in isolation from non-Christians.

The sad truth is that many professing believers have no real relationships with non-believers. If we are going to disciple our children, we must not isolate them from the reality of a lost world. Many of us see isolation from secular society as essential to our children's spiritual and moral purity, and there is certainly some truth to this, especially at younger ages. But the biblical call is not to raise children in sealed Christian communities so they can grow up and raise children in sealed Christian communities. Our goal is to reach the lost, and to reach them we must interact with them. At some point we must expose our children to the larger world. What better way to do that than to build a family culture in which you interpret and critique the larger world for your children at their various stages of development? For that to happen, you must be focused on seizing real-time teachable moments.

These are the moments that allow us—and sometimes force us—to deal with issues related to morality, truth, ethics, or a Christian worldview. I vividly remember working through the theory of evolution with my Dad after being ridiculed in my 10th grade biology class when I stated my belief in a literal six-day creation. This was a real-time issue that required discipleship.

As parents we should be less concerned overall with *whether* our children are exposed to non-Christian influences and more concerned with *what* we do about it when they inevitably are exposed. Let us seize those moments and convert them into discipleship opportunities. That is how Christians are prepared to make an impact on secular society.

When I was a child, my parents were involved in ministry to a family in which the husband was an alcoholic. They made sure I understood the dangers of alcoholism, not by setting arbitrary rules, but by allowing me to see the devastation alcoholism can bring to a family. As a result, when I had opportunities to drink in high school, I wanted nothing to do with it! My parents had taught me the kind of lesson that can only be learned in the larger community.

Sphere Three: The Church
The third sphere of family discipleship is the local

church. It is crucial for the church and home to foster a partnership in family discipleship. I want you to understand some of the essential ways the local church can help you raise children who set their hope in God and treasure Jesus above all things.

Covenant church membership. One of the biggest issues I encounter with families today is a lack of commitment to a particular body of believers. Fathers seem content chasing their kids around to the church of their choice, rather than leading their families to commit to a local church. The fact of Scripture is that a church is not a place we attend, but rather a people who covenant together to be the visible body of Christ. I believe one of the most damaging practices today is rampant church-hopping. You will teach your children a great deal by committing to a local body of believers.

Worship together as a family. Another issue in the local church today is the notion that children need to attend their own age-appropriate children's service. To the contrary, I believe it is vital for the purpose of family discipleship for your children to worship with you in the corporate gathering. I believe this for several reasons.

First, children need to sit under the preaching of the Word. The main argument against this is that most of the sermon will be over their head. This may be true, but we must also consider that preaching is not primarily didactic in its function. God intends for his people to sit under the authority of his Word as an act of worship, with the purpose of going out into the world in obedience to the Word as it has been proclaimed. Now here's the missing link—to the extent that the sermon really is over a child's head, it is the job of fathers to take that message, interpret it as necessary, teach it, and apply it in the home so that all members can gain something from it.

Second, children need to learn how to listen to sermons. When our daughter was five she began attending worship with us. She was just learning to write so we began teaching her how to take some simple notes during the sermon. She would get one "point" for each note she wrote down, even if it was just a single word. When she accumulated 20 points she would get a prize. It wasn't long before we had to increase the point total to 50 because we were buying prizes each week. Now that she is older, she gets a point for each complete note she takes in sentence form. This helps her to learn how to listen to sermons.

Third, children need to see the body of Christ gathered and participating in worship. I believe children are greatly influenced by witnessing the singing, giving, Bible reading, and sharing that takes place during worship. They may get the wiggles. They may get talkative. But the payoff spiritually will be much higher than sending them to a service where most in attendance are unbelieving children.

View church ministries as a support system.
Many churches have a wide variety of ministry
options for your family to plug into. While this is a
good thing, it does not mean your family has to opt
into every ministry in order to be faithful members
of the church (and I say this as a lead pastor). You
should view the available ministries as a support
system for your own discipleship efforts. It is very
easy to have your week so filled to the brim that
there is no time or energy for family discipleship.
Get involved with church ministries, but not at the
expense of your family.

The local church is a vital sphere in the family discipleship process. As a matter of fact, you cannot truly
be a disciple of Christ without a local church. Christ
died for his Bride, the Church. How can anyone claim
to be a disciple who does not love the church? Teach
your children to love and value the people of God.

Sphere Four: The World

The final sphere of family discipleship is the
world—every tribe and tongue and nation. We must
teach our children to love the nations as Jesus loves
the nations. There are several fun ways to incorporate the nations into your family discipleship.

One great idea is to work with your church
to plan a family mission trip. If that is out of the

question, get a few families together and plan your own trip, or begin saving now to send your children on a trip with a missions agency at some point. I had the opportunity to go to Brazil the summer after I graduated high school. The month I spent there with missionaries was life-changing.

Another way to disciple in this sphere is to pray regularly for missionaries and people groups. Pick a handful of missionaries that your church or denomination supports and begin praying for them every day. "Adopt" an unreached people group and pray for a church to be established among them. There are several prayer guides available to help you pray for missionaries. Many missionaries today also have Facebook pages or other electronic means to communicate about urgent needs and to give ministry reports. There has never been an easier time in history for families to connect with missionaries.

Giving is a powerful teaching tool that can be used to disciple your children to love the world. For one dollar a day, a family can give $365 dollars a year towards missions. There are hundreds of ways to support missions financially. Think about how effective it would be to give up a particular luxury as a family in order to provide resources to get the gospel to the world. I know families who have given up Christmas presents, television for a year, or a family vacation in order to give to missions. This type of commitment can have a life-long impact on your children.

A more radical approach to discipleship might be to adopt a child from another country. This may be radical, but it is certainly biblical! I can think of very few actions that would serve as a better tool of teaching the love of Christ for the nations than to adopt a child from a foreign land.

I hope you can see, after considering these four spheres, that the opportunities for delivering the content of family discipleship are almost endless. These ideas I've presented here are just the tip of the iceberg. My prayer is that you will add your own ideas to this list and that intentional discipleship in your home, community, church, and world will become the norm for you and your family.

Now Make It Stick:

1. List some of the ways that your children are influenced every day by secular culture. How much time are you spending investing in their spiritual growth and development in comparison?

2. Think about the various rhythms of family life as they pertain to the spheres of Home, Community, Church, and World. What are some common events that take place in each

sphere—on a daily, weekly, monthly, or yearly basis—that might be captured for family discipleship?

Home: Daily: (e.g., meals)
  Weekly: (e.g., Saturday night before church)
  Monthly: (e.g., family game night)
  Yearly: (e.g., birthdays)
Community: Daily: (e.g., drive to school)
  Weekly: (e.g., grocery shopping)
  Monthly: (e.g., youth event)
  Yearly: (e.g., Christmas parade)
Church: Daily: (e.g., conversation with believers)
  Weekly: (e.g., corporate worship)
  Monthly: (e.g., ministry opportunities)
  Yearly: (e.g., Easter service)
World: Daily: (e.g., watch the world news)
  Weekly: (e.g., missionary email updates)
  Monthly: (e.g., missions offering at church)
  Yearly: (e.g., mission trip opportunities)

3. Brainstorm some specific ideas for investing in your children spiritually that coincide with the rhythms that take place within each sphere of family discipleship:

Home:

Community:

Church:

World:

Five
THE BEDROOM

Speaking to Our Children's Hearts

The kingdom of heaven is like treasure hidden in a field, which a man found and covered up. Then in his joy he goes and sells all that he has and buys that field. (Matthew 13:44)

If I could calculate all the hours I spent in my bedroom as a child, I'm afraid of exactly what I would find. Besides sleeping in my room, I played in my room, spent hours listening to really bad synthesizer rock, organized countless piles of baseball cards, and daydreamed of pitching for the Kansas City Royals. My bedroom was a place of escape, mostly from my younger brother. It was my realm and it was there that I could be completely myself.

As we consider family discipleship, The Bedroom symbolizes the hearts of our children, who they really are at the core of their being. Before our children are born again, the Bible says they are by nature children of wrath. Their foolish hearts are darkened and hard as stone. They truly cannot know God, and are lost and without hope in this world. Perhaps more than anything else, intentional parenting is a matter of reaching the heart.

In this chapter I want to help you see the ultimate aims of family discipleship. I want you to understand the heart issues behind all of the teaching, instruction, and modeling that is required to effectively raise your children in the nurture and admonition of the Lord. It is crucially important for us to disciple our children with the right goal in mind.

What is the Goal of Family Discipleship?

Jesus used parables as powerful tools to convey spiritual truth. One of his most illustrative parables is found in a single verse, Matthew 13:44, "And the Kingdom of heaven is like a treasure hidden in a field, which a man found and covered up. Then in his joy he goes and sells all that he has and buys that field." This simple parable helps us understand the goal of family discipleship.

Reveal hidden treasure. The first truth that strikes me in this passage is that the Kingdom of heaven is likened to a treasure that is *hidden*. The parable suggests that this treasure is not self-revealing, not sitting out in the open. In fact, the owner of the field has no idea the treasure is even there. It is hidden.

Because this treasure is hidden, our children do not know it exists. And they never will unless it is somehow revealed. Why did God give children to you, a Christian parent? So that you can show them what you have learned—you know where the treasure is buried! In all your parenting—all the methods, all the techniques, all the resources—always keep in mind that your goal is to reveal to your children the Kingdom of heaven. This Kingdom represents the rulership of God the Son. You have been tasked to deposit within their hearts a vision of the glory of God in Jesus Christ. Our treasure is Jesus, Lord of the Kingdom of heaven. To reveal the Kingdom is to reveal its King.

Spend wisely. Second, this man sells all he has in order to take ownership of this treasure. He sells everything! Jesus made a habit of telling people he was worth everything. He said things like, "If anyone wants to follow me, he must hate his family in comparison to his love for me," and "If anyone wants to be my follower, he must be willing to lose his own life." Jesus made it very clear that he was worth *everything*.

So in the parable, the worth of the treasure must have been obvious and undeniable, but it wasn't just the monetary value that we should consider. By selling all he had, this man radically changed his lifestyle. He wasn't just exchanging one set of material possessions for another. He was altering what his daily existence was built around. For him, life was no longer about the things he used to own—what they meant to him and what they made possible. His life now revolved around this field and the treasure it held. The treasure not only cost everything. It redefined this man's life. The treasure changes everything.

Spend joyfully. Third, notice that the man could not own the treasure without purchasing the field, yet he did so *joyfully*. Wouldn't you have wondered what he was doing? The treasure was hidden, so the question on people's minds would be: "What was so valuable about a field that this man would suddenly turn his life upside down to obtain it? Why do this for a plain old field? And why be joyful about it?"

Of course, what others couldn't see was the one thing that made the field special. What was seen was not very compelling, but what was unseen was invaluable.

Such is the Kingdom of heaven. When we discover Jesus as our treasure, we will do things that seem irrational to the world, and we will do them out of joy. What does this have to do with family disciple-ship? It is vital that family devotions, prayer, Scripture memory, singing, and going to church are seen not as your duty, but as your delight—a delight based on your knowledge that the treasure you have found is far greater than anything else. Christ is our treasure, and the practice of our Christianity is the field. If Christianity is for you only a set of dutiful religious habits, your children will see nothing but the field. They won't understand why you have given so much to own so little. Let your joy help them see that in this field is the greatest of all possible treasures.

And here we come to the crux of the matter; the goal of family discipleship is to raise children who treasure Jesus above all things.

The man in this parable did everything in his power to have the treasure. Are we doing everything in our power to have Christ, to treasure Christ, to exalt Christ, to go after Jesus? When all is said and done, every ounce of energy that is spent in discipleship is wasted if we do not turn the hearts of our children toward Jesus as their greatest treasure. When your son or daughter is lying in bed at night, who or what is their greatest treasure? The goal of family discipleship is that at some point on their journey, their all-surpassing treasure will become and remain Jesus Christ.

As I mentioned earlier, I can remember like it was yesterday how Jesus revealed himself to me as Savior. I truly believe that God saved me at age six, but it was the continued sanctifying work of the Spirit that led me to treasure Christ more than anything in this world.

By the time I was seventeen I still wanted to live for Christ—as long as it didn't interfere with baseball, especially my pitching. I read my Bible, attended youth group, and would even share Christ with classmates from time to time, but in my heart of hearts I treasured baseball and being on the mound, every eye fixed on me as I began my wind-up.

One day the most unusual thing happened. I completely lost my ability to throw a baseball with any accuracy. I started playing catch to warm up with a teammate, but I kept throwing over his head. The coach called on me to throw batting practice, but I couldn't throw a strike if my life depended on it. In the days that followed I put in extra hours, but things only got worse. I hadn't been this bad at throwing a baseball for at least a decade. God literally took away my ability to play the game I loved.

Without Christ and the loving discipleship of my parents I am not sure how I would have handled this situation, but something clicked inside me and I knew God wanted my attention. I proceeded to do something that just days before would have been unthinkable; I told my coach I was going to miss the spring tournament so I could go on a trip with our youth ministry. By that time I don't think he cared much—how much use is a pitcher who doesn't know how to throw anymore? I finished out the season on the bench and went on two summer mission trips instead of playing summer ball.

God had begun taking radical steps to change my heart, and it was through this series of events that I truly came to treasure Christ above all things. Looking back, however, the transition involved far more than losing my ability to pitch. That was a trigger event that God arranged. But what it triggered was a body of teaching stored up in my heart, teaching I had received under the discipleship of my parents. From my earliest days I had been spiritually equipped to understand what God was now trying to accomplish in my life. Because of that equipping, all it took to stop me from racing after an idol was a little divine redirection to remind me what I had begun to forget. This would have never been possible without the many years of diligent labor and investment in me by my parents.

My parents were not perfect, and my Dad would admit that he probably fed my love for baseball as much as he did my love for Christ. But never forget that God uses jars of clay to show that the surpassing treasure is from God and not from us! The goal of family discipleship is to raise your children to treasure Christ above all things. The door in is the heart.

Four Goals that Miss the Heart

Christian parents tend to make at least one of four common mistakes in molding the hearts of their children. It is crucial to notice how each of these parenting goals miss the heart transformation we are aiming for in family discipleship.

Children Who Love Me

There is an epidemic of parenting that begins with parental acceptance as the goal. The reality is that your kids have plenty of peer relationships but they only have one Mom and one Dad. The Bible calls children to obey their parents. Parents who long for approval tend to obey their children. This is not a recipe for successful family discipleship.

Children Who Love Themselves

This goal is the clarion call of a culture in which self-esteem has become godlike. Parents who raise their children with this goal teach them that their greatest treasure is themselves, not Jesus. When self-esteem is the goal it is particularly difficult to explain to kids why God would ever allow them to go through any pain, difficulty, or suffering.

The Bible rightly points out that all of us already love and value ourselves more than we ought to. The biblical call, therefore, is not that our children would love themselves more than they do, but that they would love others *as much as* they love themselves, and God even more—more than anything or anyone.

Children Who Are Moral

This may be the most pervasively misplaced parenting goal in evangelicalism. Obedience is clearly important, for the Bible repeatedly links obedience and morality with our love for Christ. The problem occurs when we see moral behavior as the *goal* of discipleship.

Student ministry has been seeding this trend for decades, as discipleship in these contexts has tended to revolve around avoiding things like pre-marital sex, drunkenness, and music that glorifies sin. The problem with this is the idea that we somehow please Christ by avoiding particularly big sins, regardless of whether we treasure Christ in our hearts. Morality that flows from a heart focused on duty cannot please God and does not please God.

God is pleased when we joyfully deny the appeals of lust, materialism, immorality, and pride *because* our true delight is in Jesus. But if our goal as parents is behavioral in nature, our children will learn to delight in themselves and their good behavior rather than in Jesus. This goal misses the point as badly as the Pharisees missed the point. When children are quite young, behavioral goals are fine. But parents must begin moving away from behavioral goals as soon as their children can begin to comprehend that living for God is about more than obedience.

Children Who Are Successful

If we could accurately survey believing households about the values that drive priorities in the
home, I am almost certain we would find academic
and athletic success at the top of the list. Christian
parents often seem more passionate about their
child's education than his or her spiritual growth and
development. In my experience, parents rarely say
No to sporting events that interfere with Sunday-
morning worship. They want their children to
achieve in sports so badly they are willing to sacrifice
the corporate worship of Jesus on a regular basis.

We need to be reminded of the words of Christ:
"For what does it profit a man to gain the whole
world and forfeit his soul?" (Mark 8:36). Paul also
chimed in on this subject when he wrote, "For while
bodily training is of some value, godliness is of value
in every way, as it holds promise for the present life
and also for the life to come…For this end we toil
and strive, because we have our hope set on the living
God" (1 Timothy 4:8,10).

If we believe the Scriptures it is easy to see that
we must not raise our children with their success as
our primary goal. We must raise them to treasure
above all things Jesus, the sovereign Savior of people
from every tribe, tongue, and nation. Our children
know what our true priorities are. If you say that
Jesus is more important than sports or academics,

but your decisions speak otherwise, they will know what you truly believe—that corporate worship is absolutely central…as long as it doesn't get in the way of anything important.

What would happen if we were committed to corporate worship in such a way that we are only absent when providentially hindered by sickness or some other emergency? We would communicate the supreme value of lifting up the name of Jesus and sitting under the authority of God's Word. I am fearful that many parents do not commit to corporate worship because they just don't treasure Jesus that much.

We can raise kids who love us, love themselves, live morally upright, and who are ridiculously successful, but if they don't treasure Christ our parenting has missed the mark. Everything we do in family discipleship must have this aim first in mind, that our children treasure Christ above everything else. He is worth it. He is the treasure hidden in the field.

Let us teach our children to treasure Christ.

How Can I Help My Children Treasure Jesus Above All Things?

When I have the opportunity to equip parents in family discipleship at my church, one truth I try to drive home is that no formula can guarantee that a child will trust and treasure Christ. You may do everything possible to lead them to this end, yet they still may walk in rebellion and willful resistance to the gospel. You can teach them all the content in the world and model the truth faithfully in front of their eyes, and yet it is possible for them to reject Christ.

Think of Adam and Eve. They lived in paradise, enjoyed the presence of God in the garden, had no experience of sin, and had zero influence from a secular culture, and yet that was no guarantee. God, in his sovereign plan for heaven and earth, determined that he would allow them to fall into sin and thereby plunge us all into the curse. As parents, we must come to grips with the fact that God may use rebellious children to sanctify us, to help us persevere in love, prayer, and longsuffering, or even for reasons we may never understand. I realize this is a Christian parent's worst nightmare, but it is a reality.

That being said, as we consider all we have learned about family discipleship, we need to keep a few more key principles in mind. I believe that parents who follow these principles are most likely to see God bless their household with generationally faithful children.

Pray

The first principle is prayer. Everything we do in family discipleship will be for naught without prayer.

Prayer is the recognition that God is omnipotent, omniscient, and omnibenevolent and we are not. We pray because God is a father who gives us everything we need in accordance with his sovereign will. The Scripture says that when we ask for something good, he will not give us a snake or a stone, but he will give us exactly what is best for us, and at just the right time. The Scripture also says that we have not because we ask not, and that often times we ask wrongly, because our true desire is to indulge our own passions.

We must be faithful to pray for our children. One discipline I have found helpful is to write on an index card various items that I want to pray for regarding my children. When I go through my index cards during my time with God I pray specifically for each child and write down new things to pray as they occur to me or as I discover them in Scripture.

It is also helpful to pray for our children in their hearing. What a blessing it must be for them to hear us call out to the living God on their behalf in thanksgiving and intercession. We cannot pray too much for our children.

Treasure Jesus Genuinely

One thing a child, and especially a teenager, can sniff out a mile away is a hypocrite. It is my feeling that many teenagers leave the church because they were forced to attend by parents who never really treasured Christ in any meaningful way during the week.

I can almost predict that your children will mirror your love for Christ, but they will take it to the next level. If you demonstrate passion and genuine commitment for Jesus, they will most likely follow after him harder and faster than you have. On the other hand, if they sense an empty, religious, Sunday-only commitment to Christ, they will chase after the things of this world with great zeal. As I said, there are no exact formulas, and the Holy Spirit works in many mysterious ways, but I have seen this happen too many times to ignore the reality.

The greatest blessing you can give your children is to treasure Jesus above all things, even above them. Is this the reality in your home? If it's not, you can confess your sin to Christ. You can flee to him. He is your advocate. Be encouraged by what John wrote, "My little children, I am writing these things to you so that you may not sin. But if anyone does sin, we have an advocate with the Father, Jesus Christ the righteous" (1 John 2:1).

Help Your Children Develop Spiritual Disciplines

Another means to help your children treasure Jesus is to teach them to develop spiritual disciplines. If you want them to be thinking about Jesus when they are alone in their bedroom, you have to help them learn how to renew their minds. As Paul said, "Do not be conformed to this world, but be transformed by the renewal of your mind, that by testing you may discern what is the will of God, what is good and acceptable and perfect" (Romans 12:2).

Teach your children from a very early age to spend time each day alone with God. Before they can read, you can help them spend time listening to praise songs or hymns sung by other children. There are many great resources for children available today. (See Recommended Reading for a sample.)

As soon as they are able, it is important for children to begin reading through the Scripture. With young readers, it is helpful to stick to narratives such as the gospels. Other disciplines your kids need to learn are prayer, giving, and listening to sermons. Anything you can begin to teach them at a young age will only help them as they mature. Model and teach these things.

When all is said and done, even though we parents play a crucial role in God's saving design, God himself must do a life-transforming work in the lives of our children. Be inspired by Paul's words to Timothy, "I am reminded of your sincere faith, a faith that dwelt first in your grandmother Lois and your mother Eunice and now, I am sure, dwells in you as well" (2 Timothy 1:5). I believe that God blesses the faithfulness of parents. My prayer is that God will use you to ignite a pattern of generational faithfulness in your home.

A Special Word to Fathers

It is vital that we take a few moments to consider the father's special role in leading the discipleship process in the home. In 1 Thessalonians 2:11-12, we find Paul equating his ministry to a father's encouragement and guidance in the life of his children. Although this passage is not written directly to fathers, Paul's usage gives us insight into how he viewed the fatherly role.

Elsewhere, Paul does address fathers in their unique role. In Ephesians 6:4 he writes, "Fathers, do not provoke your children to anger, but bring them up in the discipline and instruction of the Lord." From this we see that one way a father *can* provoke his children to anger is to *fail* to bring them up in the discipline and instruction of the Lord.

Paul also said, "Fathers, do not provoke your children, lest they become discouraged" (Colossians 3:21). Some translations use the word *exasperate* instead of *provoke*. Here we see that fathers are to be encouraging in their instruction. Both the failure to instruct and a heavy-handed approach to instruction can create discouragement in children.

Paul treated the local churches he interacted

with in such a way as to provide an example of how to encourage each other to live as Christians. This example certainly extends to fathers as they attempt to lead lovingly in the home. Overall, in Paul's letters we see him stressing the importance of encouragement *and* instruction, for both are necessary if fathers are to parent their children successfully.

The book of Proverbs also provides an example of a father's wisdom and encouragement as it is passed down from one generation to another. In particular, Solomon speaks of the wisdom he gained from David in Proverbs 4. Now, Solomon is passing these same instructive words to his own son. This is a great example of generational faithfulness at work in the biblical record.

The Greatest Fan

Just as Paul uses fatherhood as a metaphor for his ministry, fathers should use Paul's ministry as an example of how to disciple their children. Two verbs used in 1 Thessalonians 2:12, translated in the ESV "exhorted" and "encouraged," were often used by Paul together. "Both verbs indicate the act of encouraging or cheering someone. The combination in Paul seems to indicate a positive encouragement to Christian living."[17] Through a combination of exhortation and encouragement, a father should be the greatest fan his children will ever have, as he does everything in his power to be sure they are equipped to live the Christian life as true disciples.

What does this look like? Fathers must look for opportunities to encourage their children on a regular basis, pointing out their strengths while coaching them through their weaknesses. Fathers should lead the way in praying with their children, taking their respective needs to the Lord on a regular basis. Like Epaphras, fathers should struggle for their children in their prayers, that they "may stand mature and fully assured in all the will of God" (Colossians 4:12).

Fathers cannot always be a child's best friend. But fathers can be their child's greatest fan. A father can be the one person a child knows he can always count on to be rooting him on at every stage in life. To be sure, for the Christian dad, this action is not a sentimental cheering. This kind of encouragement requires sore knees and a worn-out Bible.

The Strategic Coach

Paul uses another verb in verse 12, translated "charged." This word means to urge, and carries with it the idea of instruction and guidance. Martin explains, "*Urging* connotes the delivery of truth and was likely meant to convey the more directive functions of a father. A good father encourages and provides guidance."[18] A father who takes up the mantle of discipleship must be more than the greatest fan of his children. He must also be a strategic coach, ready and able to train, instruct, and discipline so that the children placed in his care may learn to walk with the Lord. Leon Morris rightly expounds on this passage, "But, though there is a clear note of tenderness and understanding, it is also plain that the message was uncompromising."[19]

Fathers are not training kids to win at the game of life. They are training their children to live lives "worthy of God." "It means to live in a manner consistent with the commands and character of God."[20]

It is abundantly clear what God asks of parents when it comes to the task of discipleship.

Parents today will generally do whatever it takes to see that their kids are successful in school, sports, drama, and dance. They will spend a great deal of money, time, and effort on these temporal matters. Yet very few take the time to be a strategic coach in the things of God. Fathers must take inventory of how they are preparing their children to live for Jesus. This takes both encouragement and coaching.

Now Make It Stick:

1. If your child made a list of the top-ten priorities in your home, what would it look like?

2. What do you think your current goal has been as a parent?

3. Identify three changes you can make today in your home that would encourage your children treasure Christ to a greater degree.

4. Do your children engage in any consistent spiritual disciplines? Brainstorm some ways that you can help them get started or become more consistent.

Six
TIME TO ENGAGE

Now therefore fear the LORD and serve him in sincerity and in faithfulness. Put away the gods that your fathers served beyond the River and in Egypt, and serve the LORD. And if it is evil in your eyes to serve the LORD, choose this day whom you will serve, whether the gods your fathers served in the region beyond the River, or the gods of the Amorites in whose land you dwell. But as for me and my house, we will serve the LORD. (Joshua 24:14-15)

If you have taken the time the read this book, then God is already at work in your heart. You know what needs to be accomplished in your home; it's time to engage in family discipleship! If you make this commitment, Satan will do everything in his power to preach to you and accuse you and tell you how unworthy you are to lead your family spiritually. He will call you a loser, but remember he is a liar and the father of lies. He will also tempt your children to rise up against your efforts. But remember that God has called you to this task in his Word, so you must persevere by the grace he will abundantly provide. I want to leave you with three specific challenges that I believe will help you succeed in this task.

Consecrate Your Home to the Service of the Lord

You will either have a Christian home or a pagan home. Not all Christian homes will look or function exactly the same, but Christian or pagan really are the only two options. You must either consecrate your home to the service of the Lord or disregard him to follow after your idols. A Christian home that is set apart for God will be one where the majesty and power and grace of God are treasured above all else. It will be a place where complete dependence upon God for everything is a way of life.

Joshua was a man who was enamored with the power of God. He was one of twelve spies Moses sent into the Promised Land—and one of only two who returned with a report that demonstrated faith in God's power and promises. Ten of the spies denied the power of God, but Joshua and Caleb believed God was able to defeat his enemies, just as he had said he would. We see Joshua's focus and dedication on display many years later when he stood before the people of Israel and called them to commitment, saying, "[C]hoose this day whom you will serve, whether the gods your fathers served in the region beyond the River, or the gods of the Amorites in whose land you dwell. But as for me and my house, we will serve the LORD."

If you are going to follow through with family discipleship you must apply this vital biblical principle: *God does not call us to accomplish what we can do in our own strength. He calls us to accomplish things only he can achieve.*

Do you see the task before you as unattainable in your own power? That's a good place to be.

For *you* cannot adequately disciple your children. But God wants to use you as an instrument of *his* power to accomplish his will in your home. Step one for you is to consecrate your home to the service of the Lord.

Cast Out Every Idol

When Joshua stood before the nation of Israel at Shechem he was standing on the exact spot where Jacob had cleansed his household of idols. Some of the Israelites were still harboring idols from Egypt, and Joshua knew the people would always be tempted to pollute the worship of the one true God with elements of Egyptian and Canaanite paganism. So he told them—and this is well worth repeating— "Put away the gods that your fathers served beyond the River and in Egypt and serve the LORD. And if it is evil in your eyes to serve the LORD, choose this day whom you will serve, whether the gods your fathers served in the region beyond the River, or the gods of the Amorites in whose land you dwell. But as for me and my house, we will serve the LORD" (Joshua 24:14-15).

Joshua did not allow for any middle ground. He knew that households are either devoted to God or devoted to idols, so he called for the absolute and exclusive worship of God. Some of you say that you believe Jesus is Lord, yet you hold onto your idols and serve them with more passion and zeal than you serve Jesus. What idols do you need to remove from your household in order to accomplish family discipleship? My challenge to you is to cast out *every* idol—and then do it again as often as necessary!

Commit Yourself to the Task

I love how Joshua openly and publicly committed his household to the service of the Lord and challenged the people to follow his leadership. Family discipleship is a task that I have committed myself to. I am not the perfect father; ask anyone in my family. There are many times that I want to ignore my calling from God, many nights that I just want to get the kids into bed as quickly as possible and plop down in front of the television or spend time with my wife. There are times when I fail miserably at family discipleship. But I am committed to fighting my sin and to doing whatever it takes to see that my kids treasure Jesus above all things. Are you willing to join me? Are you willing to commit yourself to this task? This is what consecration to God means. It isn't about never faltering. It's about never giving up.

In making this commitment, we are not vowing to be perfect, and there are two good reasons for this. First, we know from Scripture and experience that perfection is impossible. Second, it is not our place to commit to an outcome, for outcomes rest with God. Our place is to commit to an unwavering intention—to choose whom we will serve. Nevertheless, we must not make this commitment lightly, for devotion to raising our children in the fear and admonition of the Lord is as serious a pledge as any a man or woman can make. Count the cost, but then go after this sacred calling with all of your heart!

Commemorate Continually the Mighty Works of the Lord

At the end of Joshua 24, Joshua does one of the coolest things in all of Scripture.

> And he took a large stone and set it up there under the terebinth that was by the sanctuary of the LORD. And Joshua said to all the people, "Behold, this stone shall be a witness against us,

for it has heard all the words of the LORD that
he spoke to us. Therefore it shall be a witness
against you, lest you deal falsely with your God."

Joshua set up a stone to memorialize the commitment the people had made before the Lord.
This stone would always serve as a "witness" — a
reminder of the commitment they made. As a matter
of fact, Joshua set up seven different stone memorials,
one each to remind the people of God's faithfulness,
his judgment, his restoration, the law, his protec-
tion, unity, and the nation's commitment. I love this
practice!

If you are making a commitment to family
discipleship I challenge you to grab a stone of remembrance. It doesn't have to be a literal stone. It can be
some thoughtful gift to your family that celebrates
your commitment towards family discipleship. Make
it something special that you can display in your
home that reminds you of your commitment.

Choose you this day whom you will serve!

Now Make It Stick:

1. Write down any perceived obstacles that could
   derail your commitment to family discipleship.
   Commit to pray over these obstacles with your
   spouse and children.

Personal Obstacles:

Child's Obstacles:

Spouse's Obstacles:

2. What idols exist in your homes that need to be "cast out" in order to achieve family discipleship?
3. Plan a time of formal commitment to family discipleship. Brainstorm some ideas to make this a special event, including a "stone of remembrance" that marks forever this important decision you have made as a family.

Thanks for reading. My prayer is that this short, simple book will genuinely help you in your efforts to disciple your children for Christ. If you would like to make this more conversational, please visit me at IntentionalParentingBook.com
– Tad Thompson

ENDNOTES

1) George Whitefield, 1739. "The Great Duty of Family Religion. A sermon preached to a numerous audience in England." Early American Imprints, Series 1, no. 4450 (www.Newsbank.com/readex)

2) Sonja Steptoe, "In Touch with Jesus," www.Time.com, http://www.time.com/time/magazine/article/0,9171,1552027-1,00.html

3) Alvin Reid, *Raising the Bar: Ministry to Youth in the New Millennium* (Kregel, 2004) p 38

4) Steptoe, *ibid*.

5) Christian Smith and Melinda Douglas Denton, *Soul Searching: The Religious and Spiritual Lives of American Teenagers* (Oxford, 2005) p 270

6) Richard Baxter, *The Reformed Pastor* (Banner of Truth, 2005) p 102

7) "The Gospel Song" Words by Drew Jones, music by Bob Kauflin © 2002 Sovereign Grace Praise (BMI)

8) Mark Dever, *The Gospel and Personal Evangelism* (Crossway, 2007) p 43

9) "All I Have is Christ" Jordan Kauflin © 2009 Sovereign Grace Praise (BMI)

10) Donald Whitney, *Spiritual Disciplines for the Christian Life* (NavPress, 1991)

11) Eugene H. Merrill, *The New American Commentary: Deuteronomy* (Broadman, 1994) p 167

12) Christopher Wright, *NIV Biblical Commentary* (Hendrickson, 1996) p 99

13) Merrill, p 167

14) *Ibid*.

15) *Op. cit.*, p 170

16) Wright, p 101

17) D. Michael Martin, *The New American Commentary: 1, 2 Thessalonians* (Broadman, 1995) p 84

18) *Ibid*.

19) Leon Morris, *Tyndale New Testament Commentaries: 1,2 Thessalonians* (IVP, 1984) p 60

20) Martin, p 85

RECOMMENDED READING

Key:
+ = Good place to start   * = For children   ** = Parent/Child resource

1) The Gospel
    a. *Two Ways to Live*, Matthias Media
    b. *Two Ways to Live for Children*, Matthias Media
    c. *The Gospel and Personal Evangelism*, Mark Dever (Crossway)
    d. + *What is the Gospel?*, Greg Gilbert (Crossway)

2) The Big Story (Biblical Theology)
    a. + *According to Plan*, Graeme Goldsworthy (IVP Academic)
    b. *God's Glory in Salvation through Judgment*, James Hamilton (Crossway)
    c. *The Mission of God*, Christopher Wright (Zondervan)
    d. * *The Big Picture Story Bible*, David Helm and Gail Schoonmaker (Crossway)
    e. * *The Jesus Storybook Bible: Every Story Whispers His Name*, Sally Lloyd-Jones (ZonderKidz)

3) The Big Truths (Systematic Theology)
    a. + *Systematic Theology*, Wayne Grudem (Zondervan)
    b. ** *Big Truths for Young Hearts*, Bruce Ware (Crossway)
    c. ** *Training Hearts/Teaching Minds*, Starr Meade (P & R)
    d. Various Reformed Catechisms
    e. The Westminster Confession

4) The Great Commission
    a. *Let the Nations Be Glad*, John Piper (Baker Academic)
    b. + *Evangelism and the Sovereignty of God*, J.I Packer (IVP)
    c. *How to Bring Your Children to Christ*, Ray Comfort (Genesis)
    d. ** *Operation World Prayer Guide*

5) Spiritual Disciplines
    a. + *Spiritual Disciplines for the Christian Life*, Donald S. Whitney (NavPress)

    b.   *Five Things Every Christian Needs to Grow*, R.C. Sproul (ReformationTrust)

    c.   *The Praying Life*, Paul Miller (NavPress)

    d.   *Gospel Worship*, Jeremiah Burroughs (Soli Deo Gloria)

    e.   *Dig Deeper*, Nigel Beynon and Andrew Sach (Crossway)

    f.   *Listen Up*, Christopher Ash (Good Book)

    g.   *Literary Study Bible* (Crossway)

    h.   *ESV Study Bible* (Crossway)

    i.   ** *The Good Book Company Devotions* (Different Guides for Children/Middle School/Youth/Adult)

6) Christian Living

    a.   *Desiring God*, John Piper (Multnomah)

    b.   *The Pursuit of Holiness*, Jerry Bridges (NavPress)

    c.   + *The Cross-Centered Life*, C.J. Mahaney (Multnomah)

7) Worldview

    a.   + *Total Truth*, Nancy Pearcy (Crossway)

    b.   *Saving Leonardo*, Nancy Pearcy (B&H)

    c.   *Relativism: Feet Firmly Planted in Mid-Air*, Francis Beckwith and Gregory Koukl (Baker)

    d.   *Evidence that Demands a Verdict*, Josh McDowell (Thomas Nelson)